GILES & PIKE ARCHITE

GILES & PIKE ARCHITE

GILES & PIKE ARCHITECTS

To Mark & Katie
two of the best people I know
and fab. clients.

— Tom.

STRUCTURE AND SPACE

Artifice
books on architecture

THE GENEROSITY OF SPACE
DOMINIC BRADBURY

The work of Giles & Pike Architects is defined by a particular understanding of the generosity of space. This intrinsic appreciation of the possibilities offered by open volumes, soaring ceiling heights and a wealth of natural light lends the spaces created by Tom Pike and Matthew Giles a positive and inviting character. The introduction of double-height zones, atriums and light wells adds a sense of drama and welcome surprise to the residential projects for which the practice is best known. In this way, a house that might be simply familiar becomes extraordinary and unique.

This emphasis upon the luxury of space itself is something that can be seen across the many very different projects crafted and curated by Giles, Pike and their associates, helping to tie them together within a wide range of contexts and settings. In the case of both new-build houses and reinvented period homes, the use of open space introduces not just a generosity of spirit but a fresh focal point. In many cases, the focal point becomes a new and rounded living space. Yet in some instances the focus shifts to circulation areas such as stairwells and hallways, which become key spatial and architectural moments within the home, even within buildings of a modest footprint.

For Tom Pike and Matt Giles, architecture is about openness, volume and light with a rich sense of connection and interconnection between individual spaces, as well as constant links between indoors and out. The practice's new buildings are laid out on these principles, with a careful emphasis upon views and vistas. Yet the same ideas also apply to the challenge of updating and reinventing period houses and building stock to create spaces better suited to

Brise-soleil structure
to a glazed facade

contemporary living. The cellular, insular and formal rooms of a Victorian home, for instance, will be significantly reordered in favour of a more open and informal layout, with vivid connections formed with adjoining gardens or outdoor spaces.

The theme of spatial generosity reoccurs again and again, playing a key part in the formation of houses and homes that are welcoming and inviting, as well as being functional and practical for modern living. For Giles & Pike the focus on open space and open living is always closely allied to their interest in structure and tectonics, with space and structure forming two sides of the same coin. Although practice partners Tom Pike and Matt Giles come from two different generations, with around 20 years between them, they share very similar interests in engineering and structural solutions.

Points of inspiration include the work of pioneering American modernists such as Richard Neutra, Craig Ellwood and Pierre Koenig, as well as the British High-Tech architects of the 60s and 70s, including Richard Rogers and Michael Hopkins, all of whom focused on innovative structural approaches combined with a masterful appreciation of the innate grandeur of open space and connectivity. These lessons inform the work of Giles & Pike in many respects, while underlining the importance of the close alliance between space and structure in modern and contemporary architecture.

For Giles & Pike, the passion for structural innovation forms a guiding light. A true understanding of structure—and constant dialogue with structural engineers—lends the work a degree of tectonic ingenuity. This in turn helps to encourage the imagination, spurring a range of possibilities and helping to facilitate spaces that are a little braver and more exciting.

In some cases, as we will see through the course of this book, the structural solution—or framework—is explicitly expressed and becomes a key part of the overall aesthetic. In other instances, depending on the context, the approach may be far more subtle, with the tectonic framework discreetly presented or contained within a domesticated setting. Yet in each and every instance, this alliance between space and structure is intimate and important. It represents a modus operandi that sits at the very heart of Tom Pike's and Matt Giles' practice.

Tom Pike's route to architecture was first directed by a love of drawing and the experience, as a child, of visiting some extraordinary buildings. At school, Pike's greatest passion was for sport but a back injury as a teenager meant that he was forced to redirect his energy. During the long afternoons at his Sussex boarding school, usually devoted to rugby or cricket, Pike settled down in the art department and began painting and drawing, going on to study art as one of his A Level choices. There were no architects or designers in the family, but Pike's parents travelled widely. There were transatlantic trips on liners such as the

The entrance corridor
to Murray Road

The Generosity of Space

Queen Mary, with the great staircases and open dining rooms of the ships making a strong impression on Tom Pike as a child. The Robinsons department store in Singapore also stuck in his memory, again for the sense of space and a central atrium, which you could look across from side to side.

Back in Britain Pike also visited the Royal Festival Hall, designed by Leslie Martin and Robert Matthew. "I remember it from a very early age and still find it totally inspirational", says Pike. "I was intrigued by it as a child because of the sheer sense of space and volume, even when I didn't know what an architect was. I wasn't looking at the building through the eyes of a young architect. I was just looking at it as a child and seeing all these interesting spaces and the way that they connected with one another. It did remind me of the liners, where you also get this crossover of spaces."

Around the same time Pike's parents took him to see an exhibition at the Australian Embassy in London devoted to Jørn Utzon's designs for the Sydney Opera House. The models of the Opera House, in particular, also imprinted themselves upon his memory. Later on, while Pike was an art student at Farnham Art School, he went to visit a friend in Cambridge who took him to the history faculty library designed by James Stirling and James Gowan, completed in 1968. "Again, the whole thing is built around an atrium and the roof cascades down with these ziggurat layers of glazing", says Pike. "It has been criticised for being impractical but it is just a magnificent building."

After two years at Farnham, Pike moved on to the Kingston School of Art, concentrating his studies on interiors and furniture design, while also exploring his interest in architecture. In 1969 Pike visited a freshly built house in nearby Wimbledon that Richard Rogers had designed for his parents, forming one of his first and most influential completed projects. Partly inspired by the pioneering houses of the Californian Case Study programme, Rogers' steel and glass house was all about structure and space. A few years later Pike also visited Rogers' and Renzo Piano's Pompidou Centre in Paris while the building was being constructed, impressed by its bravery and uncompromising confidence.

Following his graduation from Kingston, Pike went to work for John Stefanidis' interior design firm, working with prestigious clients and generous budgets; one of his projects was the London recording studios of Island Records. Yet Pike realised that his interests were increasingly centred upon architecture, so he found a job with Hugh Casson and Neville Conder. "Casson and Conder were masters of detail", Pike says. "They were highly respected for producing well executed and beautifully detailed buildings. I learnt so much from them about the art of building."

Pike returned to Kingston to complete his architectural training, juggling his studies with posts at other practices, including time with architect Eric Lyons, best known for his modernist-inspired

Span housing estates of the 60s; in the late 70s, Lyons was also the president of the Royal Institute of British Architects.

"Casson, Conder, Lyons—they were all good people to work for", says Pike. "They were all generous spirited and gave you their time freely. They nurtured architects and encouraged them."

For his final diploma project at Kingston, Pike designed a speculative building on Cromwell Road, London, sitting upon the site now occupied by the Ismaili Centre opposite the Victoria & Albert Museum. The scheme suggests a powerful High-Tech influence, with its lightweight and outwardly articulated steel frame and expanses of glazing; at its heart sits a long atrium, overlooked by galleried spaces at either side and spanned by a glass roof.

In the early 80s Pike co-founded his first architectural practice with two friends and colleagues, Marvin Shane and Kathy Tilney. Much of the work from the period was commercial, with projects for galleries, publishing houses and marketing companies, as well as retail and restaurant work. It was a dynamic period in terms of pace and commissions, yet many of these projects involved 'interior architecture' rather than a structurally led approach to construction. Pike relaunched his practice as a solo practitioner, lending himself the freedom to shift direction in favour of residential new builds and conversions, which now form the majority of his workload.

"I always tend to start a project with a structural and skeletal approach", says Pike. "I am a child of the Meccano era and I guess this never quite leaves you. I can't envisage a time when I wouldn't design a building in a Meccano type way. Beams, columns, cantilevers all bolted together in an elegant way are at the heart of what we do."

A number of key projects from the 90s suggest Pike's focus on imaginative, structurally led solutions. These include Richmond Gym, a dynamic and sculptural building, where lightweight steel frames were used to create a powerful composition made up of inter-connecting shapes and volumes. This energetic dynamism echoed the purpose of the building itself, with its light, airy cathedral-like spaces serving as a training ground for a number of Olympic gymnasts.

Similarly, Pike's Asylum project in Wandsworth was guided by the ambition to create a bespoke building for a growing special effects company working in the film and television industry. The solution was a semi-industrial building, a variant on the High-Tech super shed, with an exposed steel frame and corrugated steel cladding arranged in distinctive rectangular panels.

Pike also experimented with structural innovation within a number of key residential projects of the period, most notably his new-build Weybridge house in Surrey Hills. Here, too, the High-Tech influence is apparent within a striking building that fuses the industrial and the domestic to great effect.

Around the same time Pike embraced a number of key commissions in which architecture and interior design merged at the service of creative companies seeking to express their identities through an imaginative approach to the creation and curation of their own buildings and spaces. These projects included offices for advertising agency Ogilvy's (formerly Ogilvy & Mather), the Francis Graham-Dixon art gallery in Clerkenwell and the offices of publishers Faber & Faber.

In 2008 Tom Pike went into a fresh partnership with architect Matthew Giles, marking a distinct new phase in the evolution of the practice. At the time Pike was beginning to think about the allure of creative collaboration as well as—for the future—the importance of succession planning. Matt Giles, who had already been working with Pike for some years, had just announced his intention to set up his own practice. It represented the ideal moment to join forces as Giles & Pike Architects.

Interior of Oxshott
swimming pool

The two architects certainly share much in common. Their backgrounds have a degree of similarity in that Giles, too, comes from a family without any obvious connections to the world of architecture and design. And, like Tom Pike, Giles discovered his love of architecture via his interest in drawing and fine art.

"When I went to secondary school I had a brilliant art teacher who encouraged me to draw and paint", says Giles. "The fact that he took an interest in my work gave me confidence, along with winning some art prizes at school. So I started to think about creative professions, where drawing and art would be a component part of my work, and eventually that led me to architecture."

One of the first pieces of modern architecture to make a significant impact on Matt Giles was Richard Rogers' Lloyd's Building, which he remembers from a childhood drive through the City of London with his father. Later, he visited the iconic Hampstead home of architects Michael and Patty Hopkins—a key reference point in the evolution of the truly modern British home, with an experimental steel structure that initially housed both Hopkins' office and his family.

"Patty Hopkins rather generously allowed us in and showed me around, along with a couple of student friends", says Giles. "We must have spent an hour there asking questions and taking photographs. I recall being amazed that a building could look so lightweight, almost as though it could blow away. The slenderness of those structural lines are still very impressive today."

Giles began his studies at Liverpool Polytechnic and then went on to Liverpool University. During his second year Giles visited Barcelona, which was in the final stages of preparing for the 1992 Summer Olympics, where he visited not just the Olympic Park but also the reconstructed Barcelona Pavilion by Mies van der Rohe and Josep Lluís Sert's 1975 building for the Fundació Joan Miró. Again, these buildings made a lasting impression, along with the city itself.

Between the two Liverpool courses Giles worked for an innovative practice in the city, shedkm, run by the two brothers Jonathan and Miles Falkingham. Along with Tom Bloxham, Jonathan Falkingham had also just started the development company Urban Splash and was working on one of its first residential schemes.

"They are a great firm and I was knocking on doors for a job after completing my Part One studies", says Giles. "So I joined their fledgling practice and worked on the first Urban Splash scheme, which was a warehouse conversion in Liverpool with a mix of residential and commercial spaces. It had lots of different aspects to it, which was really interesting for me as a young architect—an interesting project in an interesting place with architects who really knew what they were doing. They were impressive as a practice and made me realise that anything was possible and made me feel very optimistic about the profession, which is very important at that stage, when there's still a long slog ahead to get through your Part Two."

After graduating, Giles moved to London and took a job there for a few months with a small firm before being tempted to Miami, working on hotel projects in America and the Caribbean for three years. At the turn of the millennium he decided to move back to London and settled in to a new job with United Designers. Again, the work involved a number of hotel projects and restaurants, including a hotel in Glasgow, but there were also occasional residential commissions, including a house for actor Bruce Willis.

Ultimately Giles decided that his ambition was to lead his own projects, but he also wanted to gain experience of how a smaller practice is managed and run. He spotted an advertisement for an architect in an architectural journal and found himself being interviewed by Tom Pike. The two men established a strong connection very quickly. Following a brief look at Giles' portfolio they began to talk about other things.

"We mostly talked about books, what we were reading and authors that we liked", says Giles. "I remember talking about Mordecai Richler, a Canadian writer that I like very much, and we found that another shared interest is fine art—painting and sculpture. We both have compulsive art buying habits and my wife Liza is an artist along with my sister, Lucy."

Giles joined the practice in 2002 and became a partner in 2008. They tend to divide projects between them in terms of taking the role of the creative lead, yet they also collaborate and consult as often as time and opportunity allows. They share a common perspective and outlook, agreeing on most things, which creates harmony rather than the dialectical tension seen in some partnerships.

"We do have a very similar way of looking at the world, despite the age gap", says Giles, "and we tend to use a similar set of reference points when it comes to architecture and art. But it also made me feel so much more comfortable to embark on a new partnership knowing that I was working with someone who had already been running a practice very successfully for some time."

As well as sharing a common framework of reference points and interests, architecturally and culturally, Tom Pike and Matt Giles also concur on their list of priorities when it comes to the design process. They are firm believers in functionality and practicality, arguing that every building they design must work well and flow freely and easily. Tied to this is the clarity of layouts and floor plans, with a logical and pleasing arrangement of interconnecting spaces, while the ingredient of natural light and sunlit illumination is seen as essential.

Other key concerns include the importance of views and vistas within the building itself, along with the creation of a strong and constant flow between inside and outside space. In one way or another, all of these concerns and preoccupations are linked to the vital emphasis upon structure and space.

It is the quality of the spaces forged and crafted by Giles & Pike that matters most, in which the structural solution always plays a powerful part. A Victorian house at Felsham Road in Putney, for instance, has been totally transformed with a layered and partially double-height addition to the rear. This is much more than an extension, forming—in effect—a building upon a building, with a powerful sense of connection to the garden alongside. Bands of glazing introduce waves of sunlight to an open-plan space holding a generously scaled kitchen and dining room. The structural athletics are striking, with much of the weight of the new addition taken invisibly to the side walls and almost nothing—barring one modest pillar—in the way of visible columns and supports.

At Sewdley Street, in Hackney, north London, a former workshop dating from the nineteenth century has also been reworked and reinvented through a positive and imaginative structural approach. An insular, box-like and somewhat dysfunctional building has been given a new lease of life with the introduction of a layout arranged around a concrete spine and a top-lit staircase arranged on the diagonal. This new backbone has released the potential of the house, with a more dynamic floor plan, while also serving as a light well. New connections have been forged between interior and exterior spaces and an additional storey added.

The front facade at
Sewdley Street

The Generosity of Space

In certain cases the structure becomes a key part of the overall aesthetic approach and character of the building, as seen in Giles & Pike's Highfields Pool House. The demands of the budget and site led to a semi-industrial solution for the single-storey pavilion, with a lightweight steel frame—featuring perforated beams for a lightness of touch—and extensive glazing. The High-Tech influence upon the Pool House is evident.

At times, challenges in terms of site, context and budget can drive solutions that are both imaginative and dynamic. In Wandsworth, at Amerland Road, Tom Pike spotted an opportunity to build a modest but inventive house on a backwater plot at the end of a garden. The timber-clad building, on a tight footprint, is a delight and full of spatial and structural ideas that make the most of the available space and light. An open-plan kitchen and dining room area is positioned at ground floor level, leading out to a small secret garden, while a large sitting room is situated on the level above, illuminated by a large skylight. These two levels are interlinked by a double-height atrium, adding to the sense of volume and allowing light to circulate, while two bedrooms and bathrooms are tucked away at lower ground level, illuminated by light wells.

A delightful mid-century house at Murray Road in Wimbledon offered Giles & Pike an opportunity to pay honour to a striking example of 60s architecture by Peter Foggo, while adding a sympathetic and sensitive addition of their own. Here, again, structure and space are everything. Foggo's original single-storey house uses a combination of concrete 'goal posts' and steel framework, plus extensive glazing, to create a fluid and graceful pavilion. Giles & Pike have fully respected the character and intent of the original building in their restoration and updating of the original design, while adding a new wing of their own to create an L-shaped home arranged around a courtyard garden, with vibrant interaction between outside and in.

The Wimbledon house neatly connects back to many of the themes and influences already discussed, echoing in some ways the look and feel of the Californian Case Study houses and also linking with some of the preoccupations explored by Rogers and the High-Tech pioneers. It is clearly a project that also delights Tom Pike and Matt Giles equally, layered as it is with art and ceramics, plus a rounded and characterful garden design.

It is a project that underlines the idea with which we began: the generosity of space. This is a home full of connections and vistas, where each space leads gently and gracefully into another within a gentle journey of discovery. It is a generous and open house, created in a spirit of fruitful collaboration, made possible by a thoughtful approach to structure. As in so much of Giles & Pike's work, there is a note of welcome surprise as you begin to enjoy the sense of space and start to appreciate the layers of thought behind such a rounded and complete home.

Basement entrance at
Broomwood Road

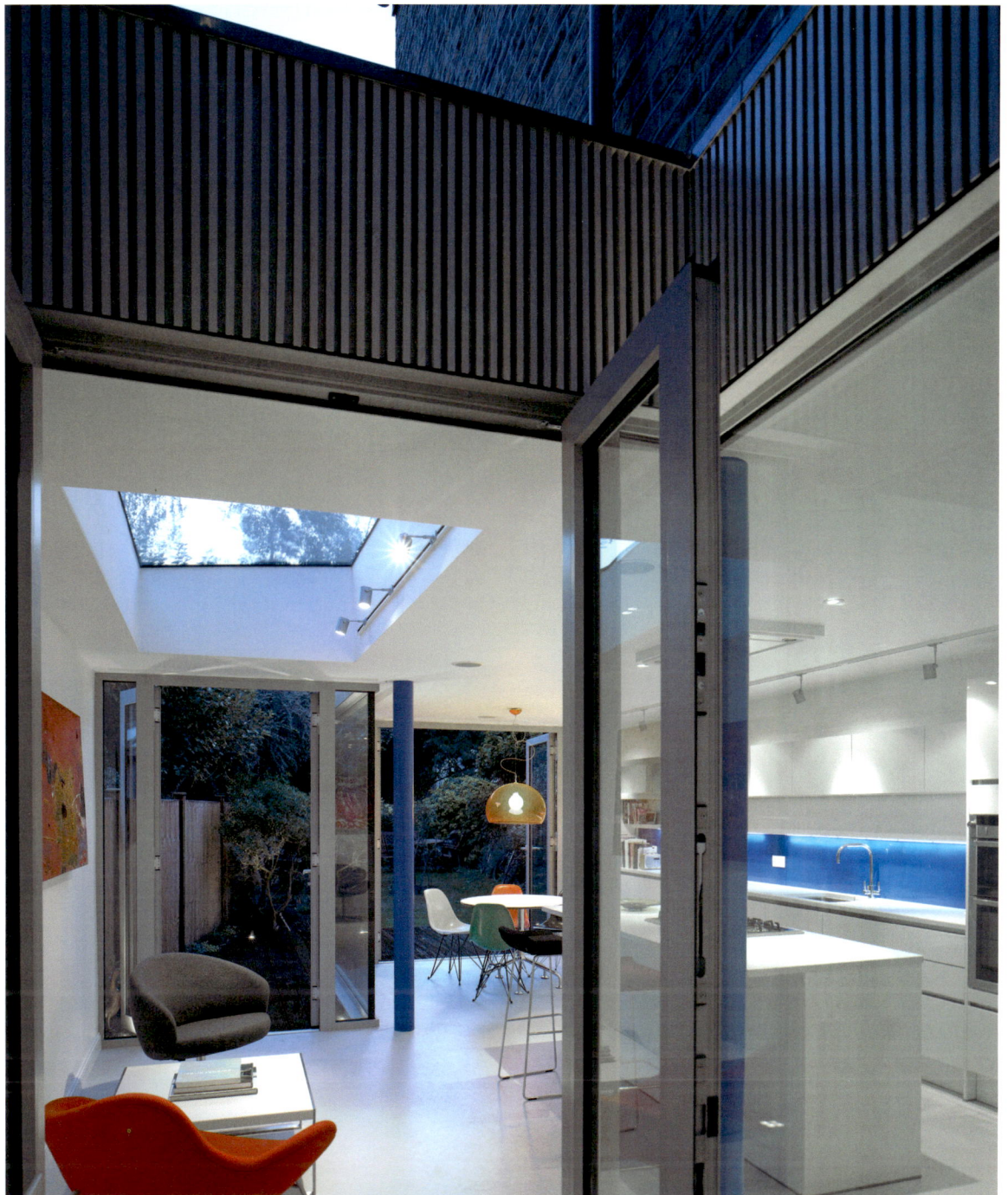

View from the inner
courtyard at Melody Road

Entrance courtyard
at Murray Road

STRUCTURE AND SPACE

TOM PIKE

The buildings that we love and the buildings that fire our imagination are more often than not buildings with a strong structural expression.

As we enter these buildings, we tend to look upwards and marvel at the space above us and the way that space is framed and supported. A clear and well-defined structure not only gives confidence and comfort, but also satisfies and causes delight.

As an architect, I have always been inspired by buildings where there is evidence of imaginative and heroic engineering. I have always admired engineers who design architecturally, and architects who design with engineering as an intrinsic part of their design process.

Across Europe and the Americas, there is a rich history in terms of engineering-led architecture and architecturally led engineering projects. Looking at our heritage, so many names pop into our consciousness, starting with Thomas Telford in the eighteenth century, who was such a pioneer in the use of iron, and who literally forged the architecture of the Industrial Revolution. Moving forward into the nineteenth century, there were Joseph Paxton and Isambard Kingdom Brunel, who gave us groundbreaking structures and techniques, and who were both men with immense entrepreneurial verve. Then in France, Gustave Eiffel designed the Eiffel Tower at the very end of the nineteenth century, one of the most dynamic and eye-catching structures of all time.

In the United States, Louis Sullivan virtually invented the concept of the 'sky scraper' at the beginning of the twentieth century. As well as working out how to design very tall buildings and to deal with massive wind loadings, he was also an innovative designer who coined the maxim "Form follows function"—something that is at the centre of our philosophy at Giles & Pike Architects.

Returning to Britain, Giles Gilbert Scott successfully and majestically combined architecture and engineering and produced a string of awe-inspiring power stations. Tate Modern now benefits from one of these at London's Bankside. Sir Ove Arup, a Danish/British engineer who founded and developed the most successful of multidisciplinary practices, amalgamated architecture, art and design with all the engineering disciplines. Arup Associates have been responsible for so many great projects in the twentieth century, the most celebrated of all being the Sydney Opera House, where he worked closely with the architect Jørn Utzon to produce a building that really did bring Australia immense prestige. Has ever a building acted as such an emblem for a nation?

In Brazil, Oscar Niemeyer designed many of the buildings in the new political capital, Brasília. His buildings are totally expressive and sensuous, and they all have bold and iconic engineering as the essence of their design.

From the early to the middle half of the twentieth century, a French artisan metalworker, untrained as an architect or engineer, started to work with both architects and engineers to produce the most spectacular buildings and components. His name was Jean Prouvé and he was responsible for creating that brand of French engineering that is regarded with so much affection—eg the 2CV car and the Citroen H van with corrugated steel side panels. Prouvé's work was inventive and informal in style. He was greatly admired by architects, including Le Corbusier, and was invited by both architects and engineers to collaborate on construction projects. For me personally, the freshness and directness of Prouvé's designs have always been an inspiration... the 'anything is possible' mentality is so enticing and gives one so much hope.

During the latter half of the twentieth century, a generation of young British architects emerged to design dynamic buildings with expressive structural designs. I refer, of course, to Richard Rogers, Norman Foster, Nicholas Grimshaw and Michael Hopkins, with Ian Ritchie and Richard Horden coming close on their heels. These architects, all roughly of the same age, and all influenced by people like Jean Prouvé and Buckminster Fuller, have changed the face of architecture in Britain and around the world.

I was fortunate enough to be an architecture student just as they were making waves and breaking onto the scene. In doing so, they were edging out the old guard of commercial architects. Through the 1980s, the architectural world changed as these architects came to prominence, and the influence of the older generation began to wane. The large commercially led firms who had enjoyed

Tom Pike's diploma project of
1978, a scheme for a new Design
Museum in South Kensington

23   Structure and Space

dominance in the 1950s, 60s and 70s started to lose out to the new talent who were coming up behind them and who were delivering spectacular buildings that caught the imagination of a nation, and helped to put Britain at the centre of world architecture.

It was this generation of architects that inspired me as a student... and they still do to this day. The notion of creating a building, whether it be a garden shed or a cathedral, that through its engineering and construction can be innovative and intriguing, is a constant challenge, and hopefully a constant opportunity.

When I was at college in the 1970s, we had a lecture on exposed steel framing by John Winter, an architect who had worked in the United States for a period in the office of Mies van der Rohe. Most of his talk was about how he built his house on the edge of Highgate Cemetery, constructed with Corten steel. To build the frame, Winter engaged the steelworkers who were striking during the 1967 Ford strike—now immortalised in the film *Made in Dagenham*. He capitalised from their position on the picket line and consequently made many new friends amongst the steel working fraternity. John Winter was an architect of the post-war era who never achieved the same celebrity status as the Foster/ Rogers generation. Nevertheless, he was an architect as inventive and resourceful as any, producing many elegant steel framed buildings. There was always a subtle economy of effort inherent in his designs.

Here at Giles & Pike Architects, my partner Matt Giles, myself and our team all share a love of inventive, structurally led design solutions, and we tend to be inspired by the same sort of buildings and the same architects and engineers. Being enthused by the work of others, both from the current generation and past generations, is a vital ingredient in our whole design process. This inspiration continues to drive our creativity into producing more interesting structures, with more generous spaces that exemplify our company ethos.

In recent times, we have all been influenced, inspired and challenged by Zaha Hadid and therefore, I end these notes by paying tribute to her. She had talent, courage and discipline in equal measure along with her magnetic personality. A larger-than-life figure in our world of architecture and design.

RECENT PROJECTS

Interior view of Sudbrooke
Road rear extension

FELSHAM ROAD

Felsham Road is a bold and radical reworking of an early Victorian semi-detached house in Putney. Giles & Pike Architects' brief was to extend and improve the property to achieve its maximum potential and in so doing, they have exploited the volume within the house to create double-height spaces. These were realised by extending the basement area and naturally linking it with the ground and first floors. The generous spaces, combined with the increased amount of natural light entering the house through large areas of clear frameless glazing, make a spectacular home equipped for modern family living.

View into the double-height
space from the mid-level platform

Felsham Road

Views across the kitchen / dining
area at Felsham Road

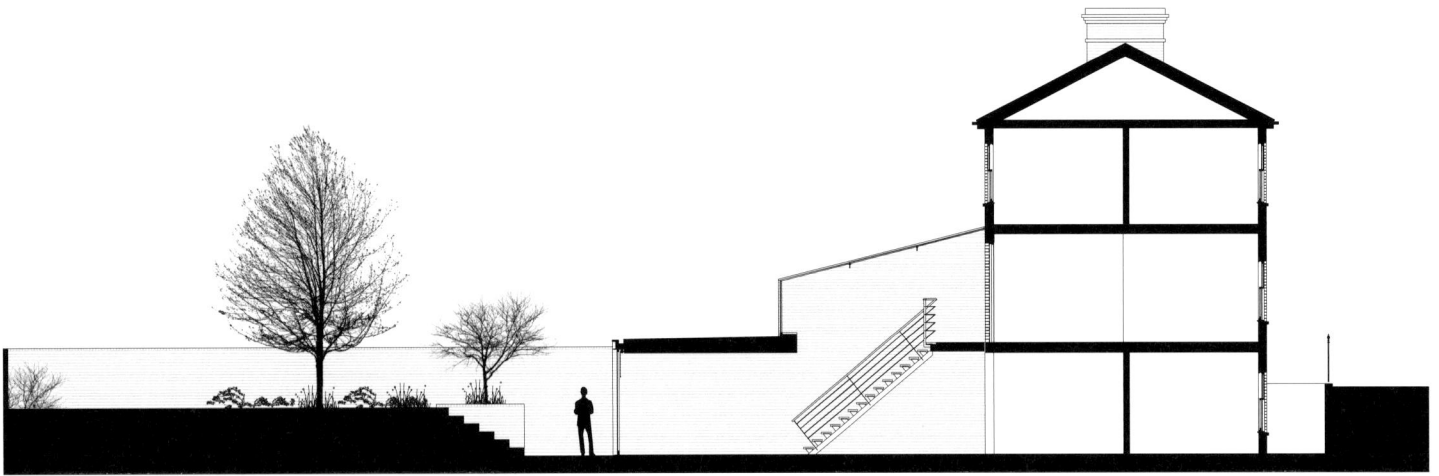

Section through Felsham
Road house

32

Landscaping to the entrance
courtyard at Murray Road

MURRAY ROAD

At Murray Road alongside Wimbledon Common, Giles & Pike had the opportunity to redesign and reinvigorate an iconic 1960s house by the architect Peter Foggo. On starting this project, they could see that the original house had become dilapidated and outdated, but its concrete structure was still sound. Giles & Pike stripped the building back to its basic structure, removed unwelcome extensions and reinvented the house, giving it a new lease of life. They also designed a new timber-clad wing that acts as a sympathetic foil to the original skeletal structure.

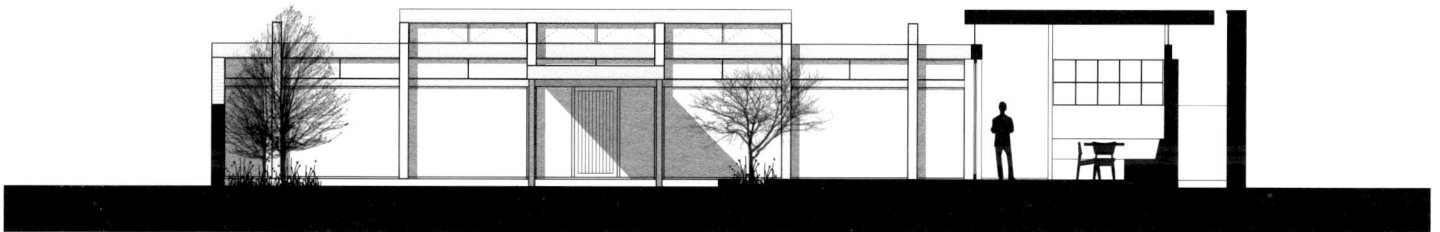

Sectional elevation of
the Murray Road house

Murray Road

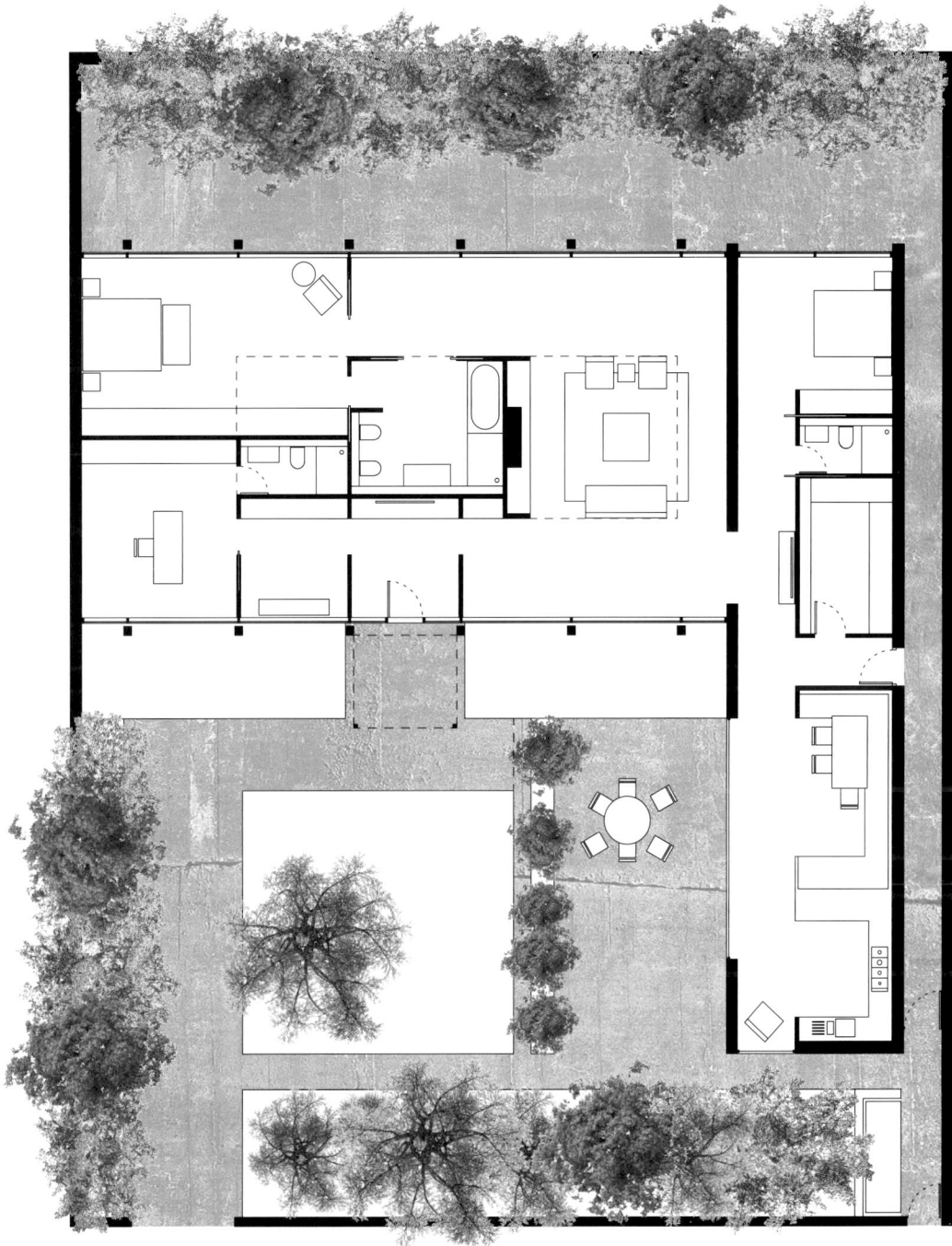

Floor plan and landscaping
at Murray Road

Murray Road

The restored concrete
structure at Murray Road

Birch veneered plywood
panelling at Murray Road

Cantilevered fireplace in
the main living room

Murray Road

AMERLAND ROAD

On a tiny patch of land occupying the border between Southfields and Putney, Giles & Pike Architects have designed and built a small yet elegant two-bedroom house over three floors. The house was designed 'in section' rather than 'in plan', maximising the potential of this restricted plot where a garage once stood. The bedrooms and shower rooms are in the basement and the open-plan kitchen and dining room are on the ground floor, with the living room and study on the first floor mezzanine that opens to a terrace and small garden. Although the house is modest in scale, they have engineered the building so that natural light permeates deep into every floor, exuding a feeling of space and comfort.

Interior and exterior views
of the Amerland Road house

Timber cladding and zinc
roofing at Amerland Road

View into the house
from the terrace

Amerland Road

Mezzanine level dining
room at Amerland Road

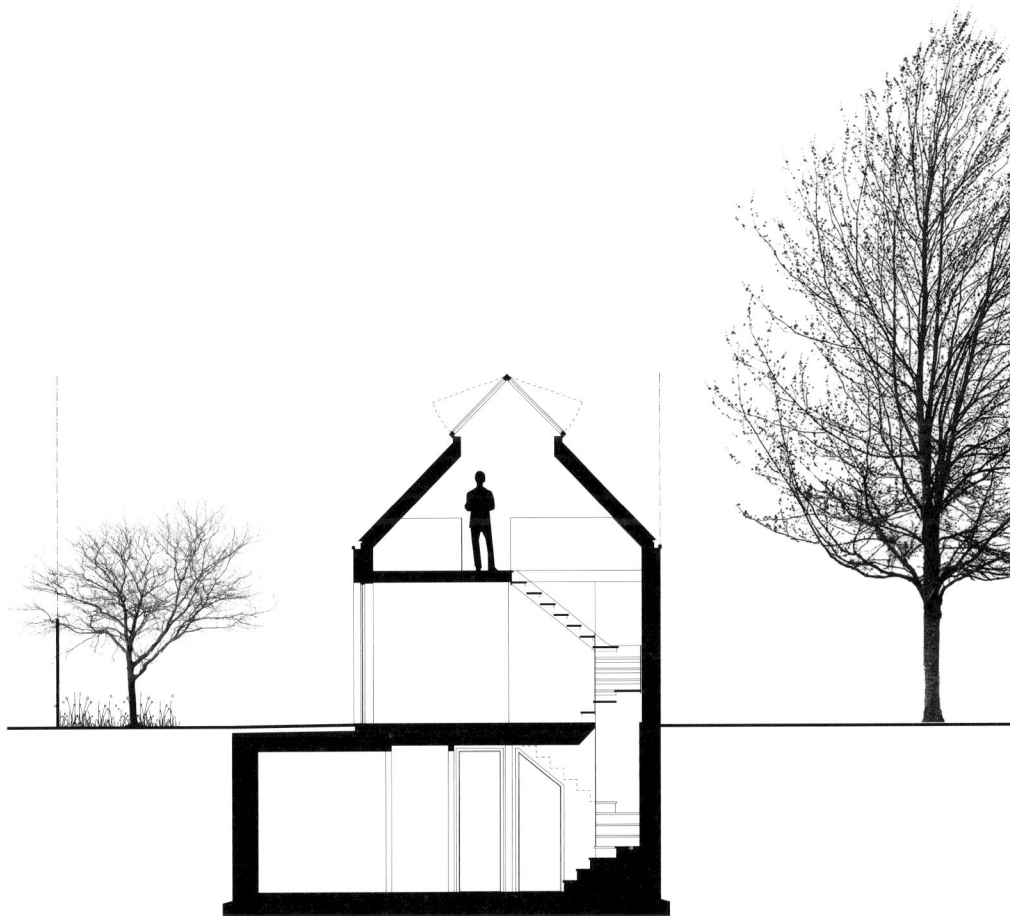

Street elevation and cross
section through the house

53   Amerland Road

Rear elevation showing the glazed
basement and glass tower at
Wandsworth Common North Side

WANDSWORTH COMMON NORTH SIDE

Giles & Pike restored and repaired the original fabric of a majestic Victorian villa located close to Wandsworth Common, adding a contemporary glass tower that has initiated an intriguing dialogue between heritage architecture and modern technology where the new meets the old. The bold glass tower has not only increased the footprint of the property but has added a fabulous contemporary twist to a house of genuine architectural interest.

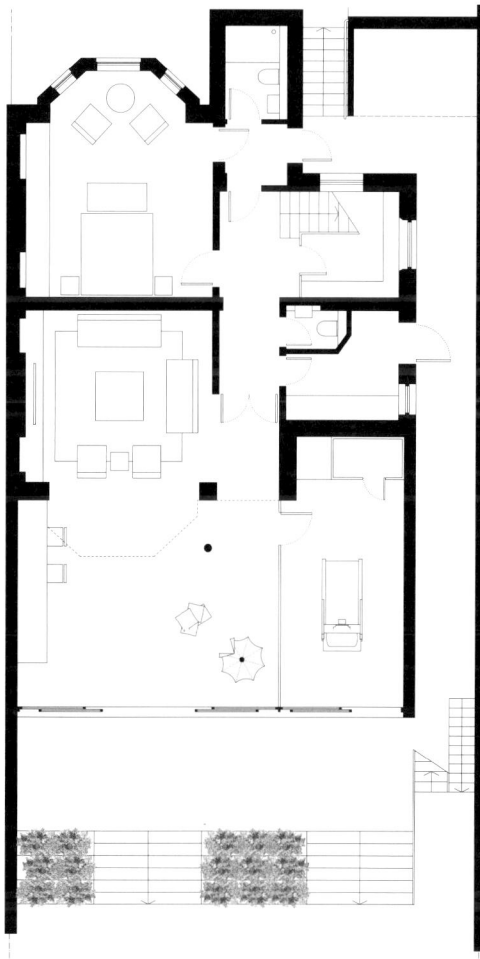

Rear elevation drawing

58

Interior views of the
kitchen / dining room

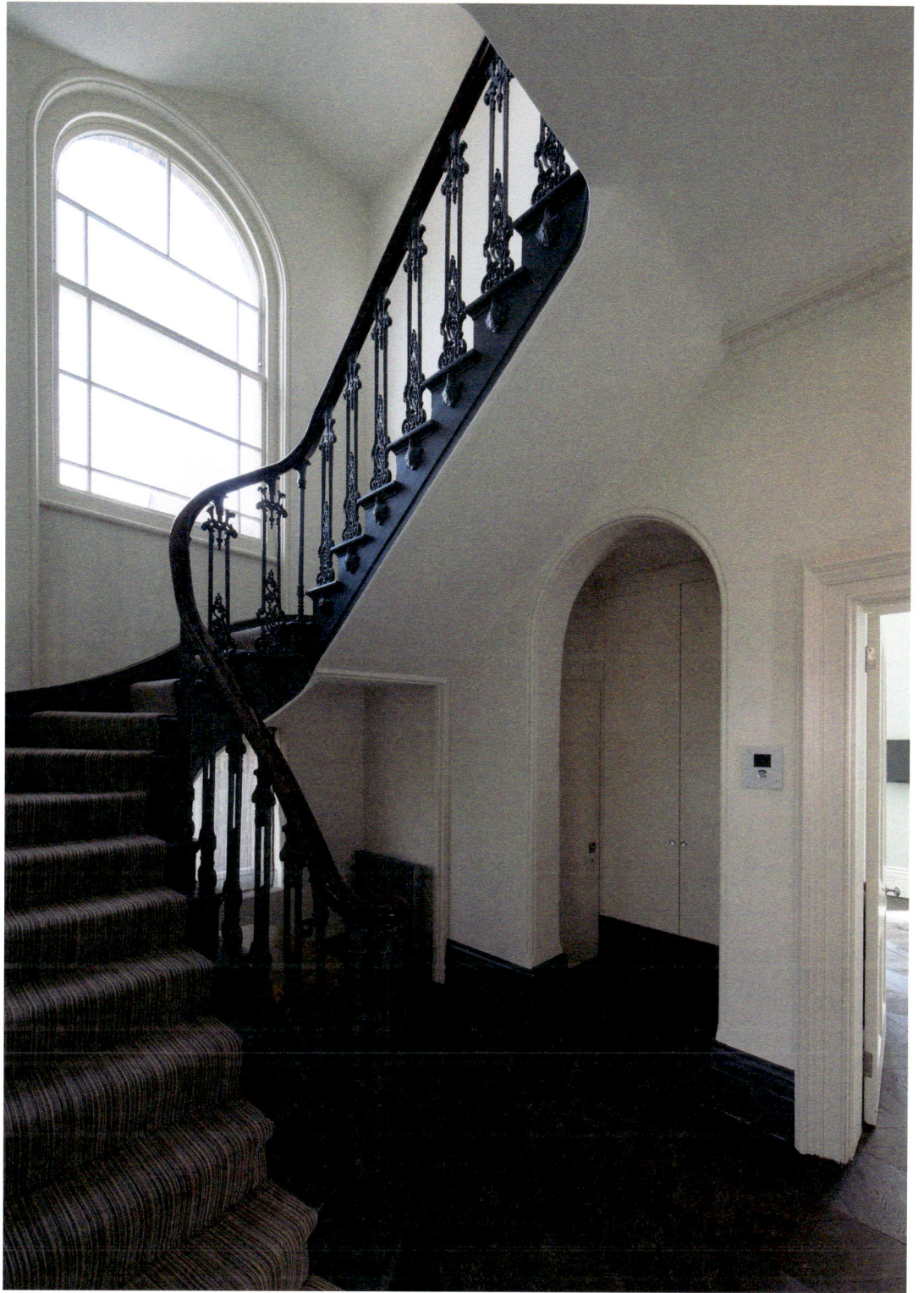

The restored staircases and
remodelled entrance hall

Wandsworth Common (North Side)

SEWDLEY STREET

In Hackney in east London, Giles & Pike have converted an industrial warehouse from a dilapidated Victorian building into a house for a young city lawyer. By transforming and extending the building, they were able to introduce a concrete wall that rises through three storeys, accommodating a new staircase of steel and recycled oak that works as the main vertical link in the house. It also acts as a prominent design statement. They deliberately maintained a limited palette of raw materials such as fair-faced brickwork, exposed concrete, steel-framed windows and recycled timber to correspond with the industrial aesthetic of the building.

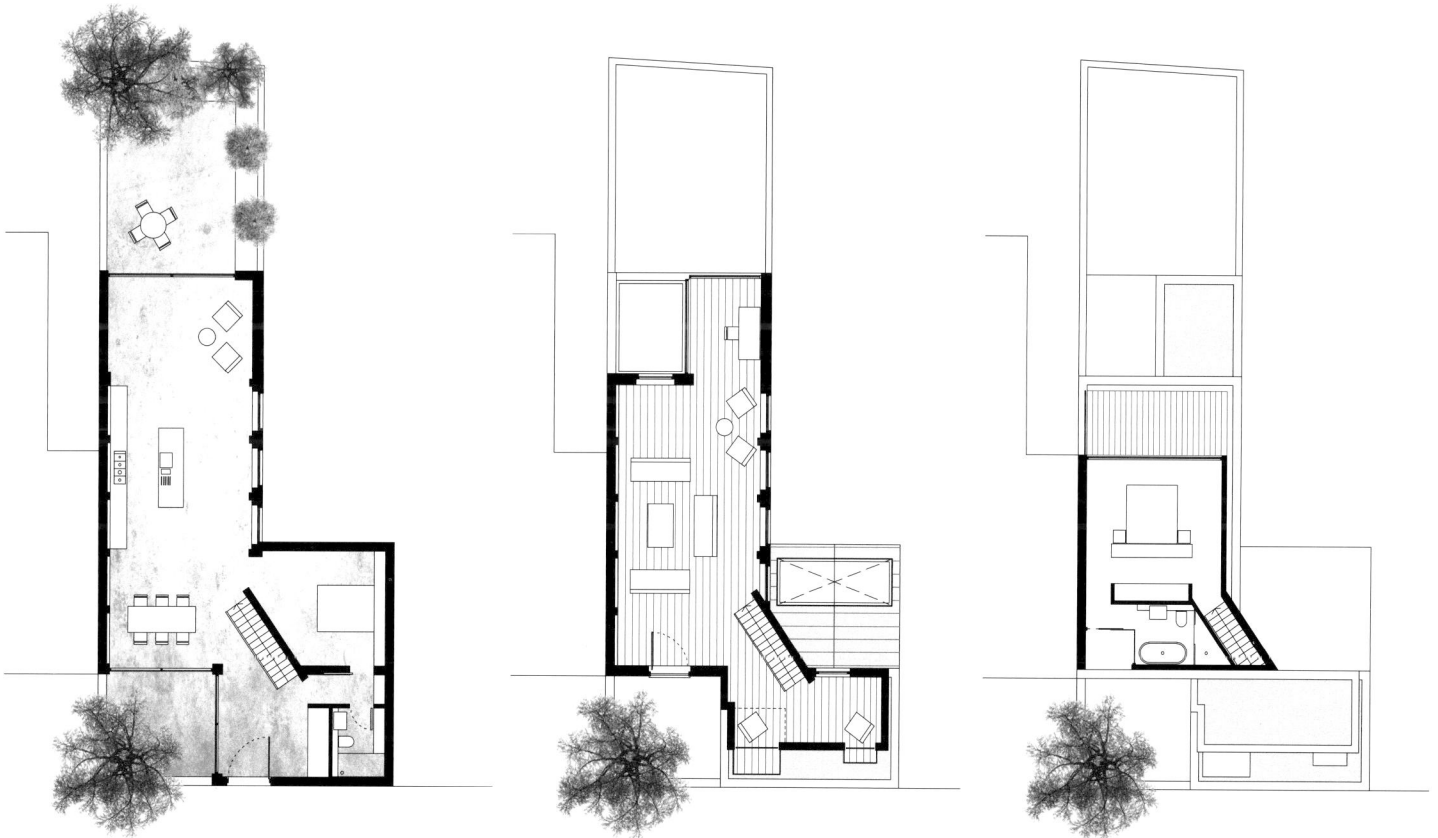

Plans of Sewdley Street house: ground floor, first floor and second floor levels

Main living room on the first floor

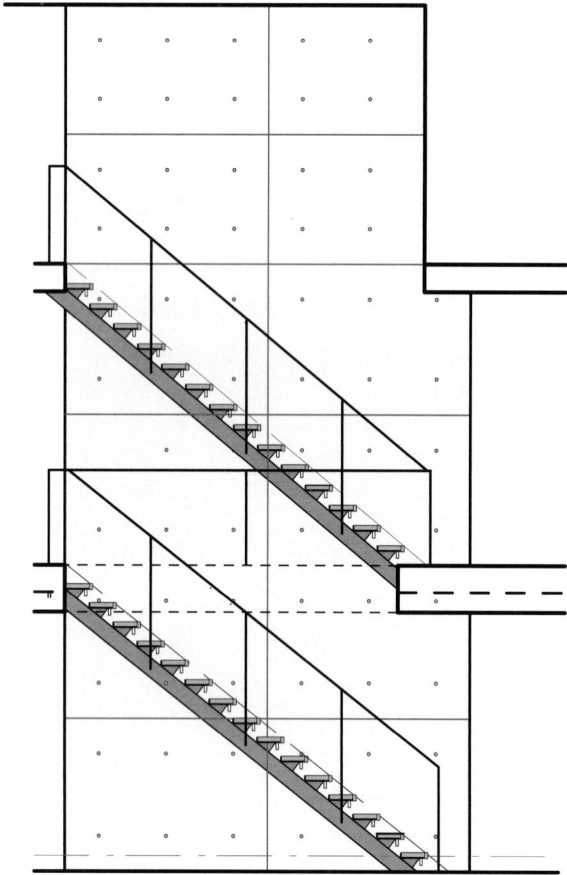

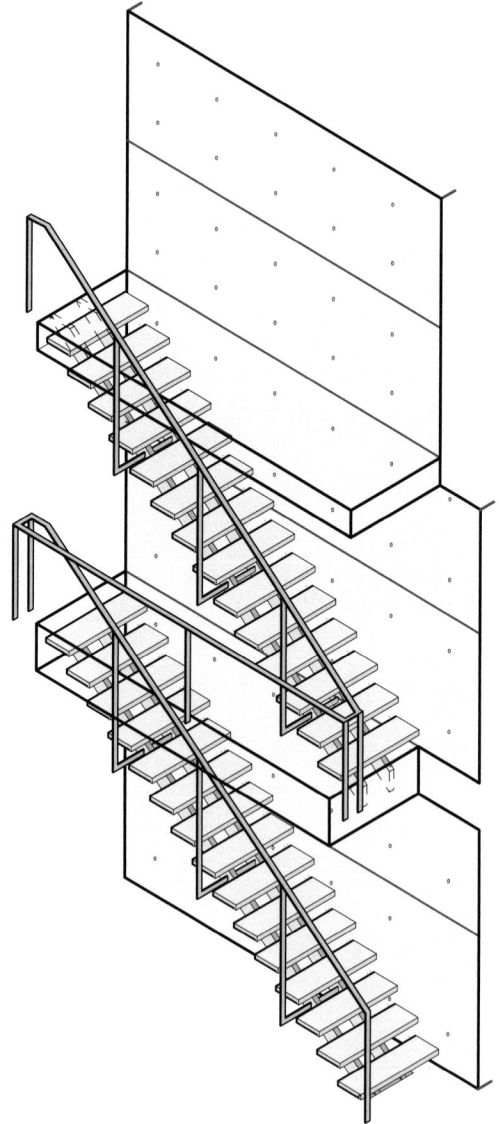

Staircase structure and
reinforced concrete wall

View from the guest room
through to the kitchen

The dining area and
entrance courtyard

Sewdley Street

THURLEIGH ROAD (WEST)

In one of the prime roads in south-west London, close to Clapham Common, a substantial Edwardian house needed complete updating for modern family life. Giles & Pike Architects' scheme not only involved the total reworking of the house but the creation of a full basement that extended under the whole property and into the rear garden. One of the outstanding features of this basement is its generous ceiling height. Rising to 2.7 metres, it gives a feeling of outstanding space and light—not at all like a basement! They then connected the new basement areas to the main living room via a stylish staircase that acts not only as a vertical link but also as a striking design feature in its own right. The house now boasts genuinely generous spaces filled with natural light and is a great venue for both family life and entertaining.

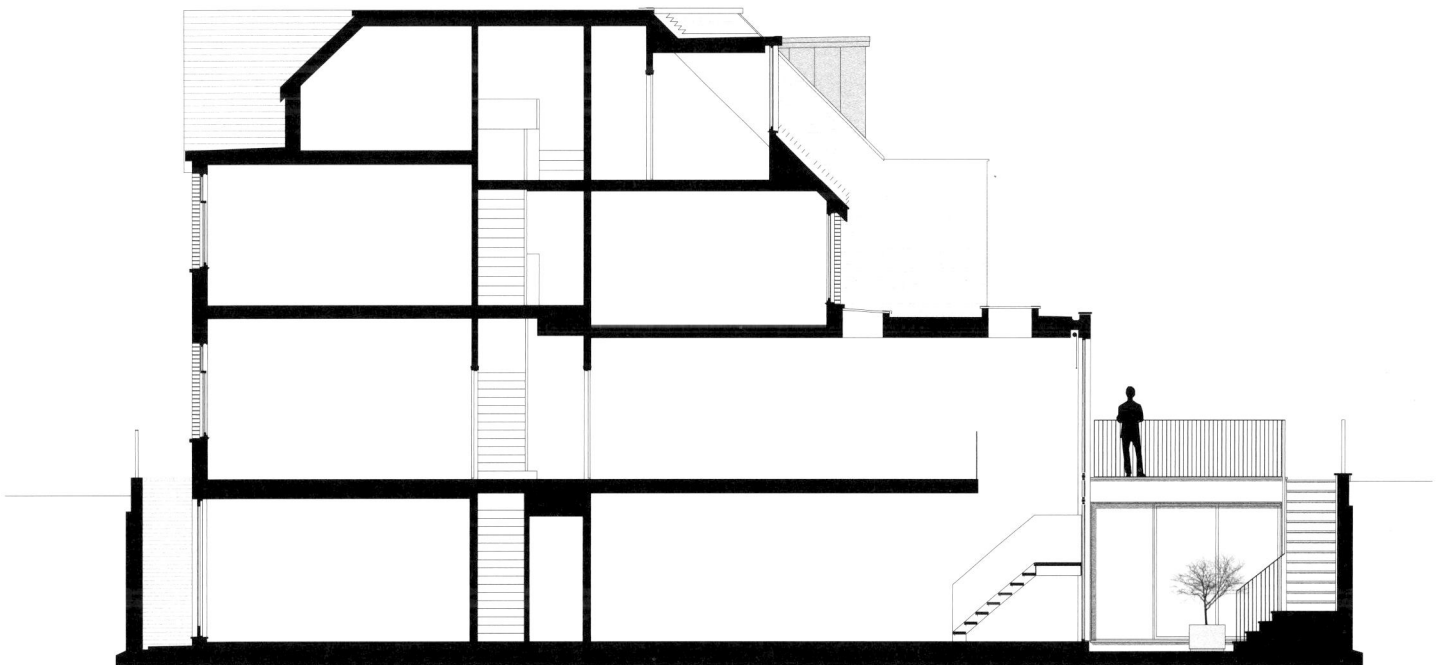

Section through the house
showing the double-height space

Thurleigh Road (West)

Views across the double-
height space and staircase

74

Detail view of the new
glass and steel staircase

Thurleigh Road (West)

View of the house from
the garden showing new
additions and glazing

Rear view of Sudbrooke Road
house, showing the new additions

SUDBROOKE ROAD

Transforming a very ordinary 1930s suburban house complete with decorative stained-glass window panels into a modernist's dream home was a gift for the architects. The client, who runs an advertising agency, was fascinated and knowledgeable about Bauhaus and the origins of the Modern Movement in both architecture and design—right up Giles & Pike's street! The client, thus, enthusiastically embraced the modernist nature of the practice's designs, which not only completely changed and updated his home but extended it as much as was physically possible—almost doubling its size.

Rear elevation drawing

Sudbrooke Road

ST MARY'S ROAD (SOUTH)

The client originally bought an existing house on a plot with the intention of carrying out a major refurbishment and redesign. However, as the project progressed and the scope of work increased, the client decided to commission a completely new house. The new-build house posed challenges for planning consent due to its location in a conservation area between Wimbledon Village and Wimbledon town centre. After a significant amount of negotiating and lobbying, Giles & Pike managed to achieve a very positive planning outcome. This new house represents a straightforward approach to inserting a strong contemporary house into the context of a conventional suburban setting. Whilst the exterior has many references to mid-twentieth-century house types, it also strikes a bold note within the conservation area.

Once inside, the house takes on a decidedly modernist feel with an emphasis on open space, light and sharp minimalist detailing. The central section of the house is a dramatic triple-height space that is bifurcated by a dynamic staircase, fabricated from steel and glass. This rises through the house and links all the accommodation within the building. This new house has been designed to be ecological and sustainable. The use of solar panels, photovoltaic cells, water storage reservoirs and high levels of thermal insulation all contribute towards a house with a very low carbon footprint.

Opposite: Dramatic staircase
at St Mary's Road

View from the garden at dusk

St Mary's Road (South)

Polished concrete island
units in the kitchen

Opposite: View into the kitchen
area from the terrace

Views across the main
living room

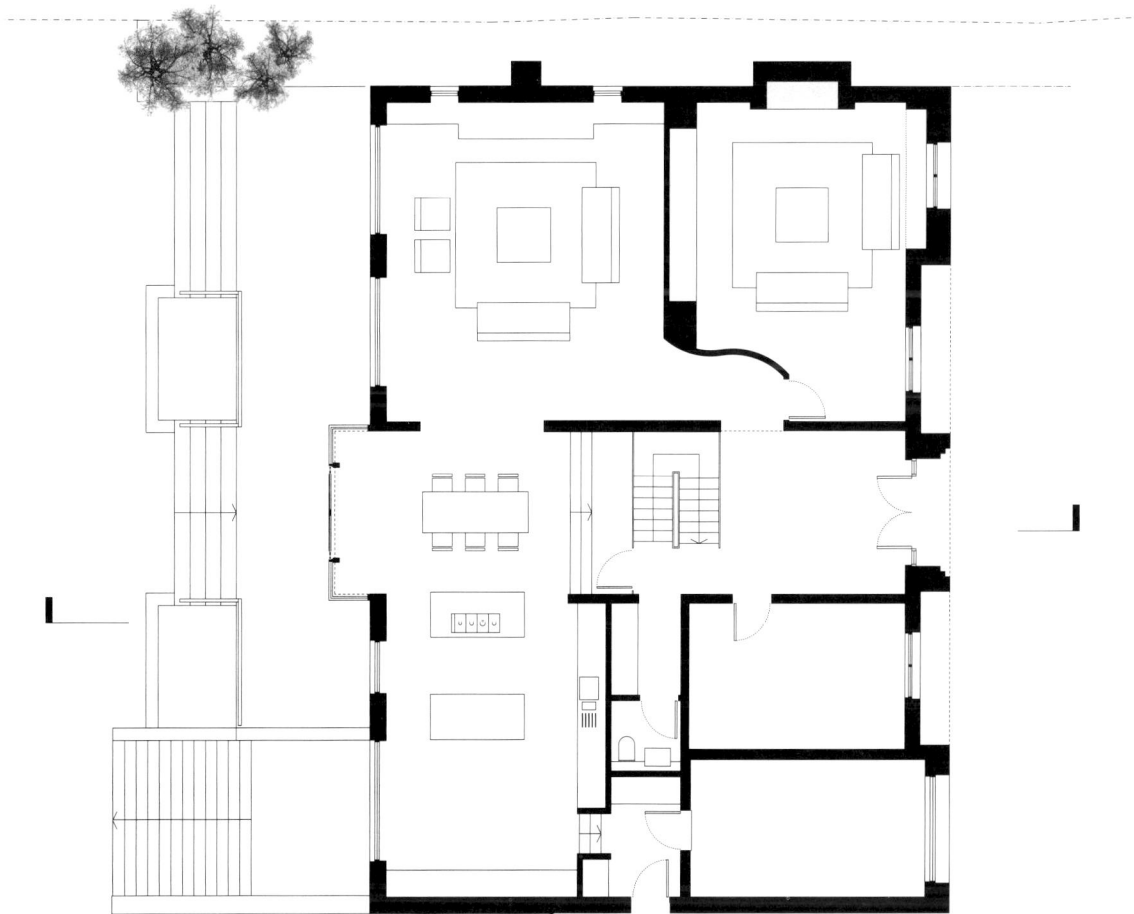

Plan and section of
St Mary's Road (South)

89

St Mary's Road (South)

Double-height dining room

90

Main entrance at St Mary's Road
(South) with projecting eaves

91

St Mary's Road (South)

OXSHOTT SWIMMING POOL

Clients of the practice whose house they had worked on in Oxshott, Surrey, asked Giles & Pike to design a new swimming pool at the far end of their garden. During the briefing and design process, the scope of work grew with the architects and client finally settling on a plan that included a gymnasium, full changing facilities and a relaxation area, as well as the swimming pool. In other words a full private leisure centre! Due to the scale of the operation, Giles & Pike Architects elected to design the new building using industrial construction techniques, thereby exposing all the steel structure on the inside. So the new swimming pool has the feel of a dynamic modern leisure centre but is located in the garden of a private home. It has proved immensely popular with friends and family alike!

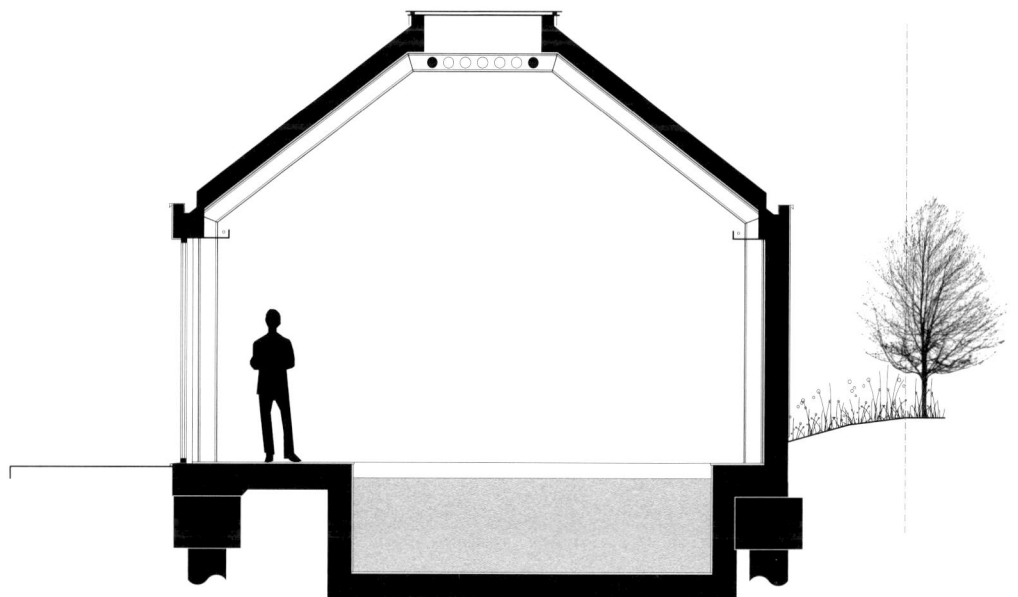

Cross section through the
swimming pool enclosure

Oxshott Swimming Pool

Cross-bracing detail to the steel
structure of the pool enclosure

ST MARY'S ROAD (NORTH)

Demolishing a house to build a new one can be the best economic solution for creating a new home. This project in Wimbledon is one such example. The new house on the original footprint makes a much better use of space and the quality of the new-build scheme far exceeds that of the earlier property. Our main achievement here was to obtain planning consent for an uncompromisingly bold design in the middle of a traditional and conservative locality.

Opposite: Front elevation to the
St Mary's Road (North) house

Cross section through the house

St Mary's Road (North)

ROYAL MANSIONS

The practice carried out a major internal remodelling of an Edwardian mansion flat overlooking the river at Henley-on-Thames. The apartment enjoys a great location and now, owing to the complete redesigning of its interior, it has a new lease of life and makes a stylish and colourful modern home. A clean colour palette has given a liveliness and freshness to the apartment that complements its natural surroundings.

Opposite: Entrance corridor
at Royal Mansions

Main living area

Main living area

Main living area

Main living area

Main living area

Views showing the floating
partition walls at Royal Mansions

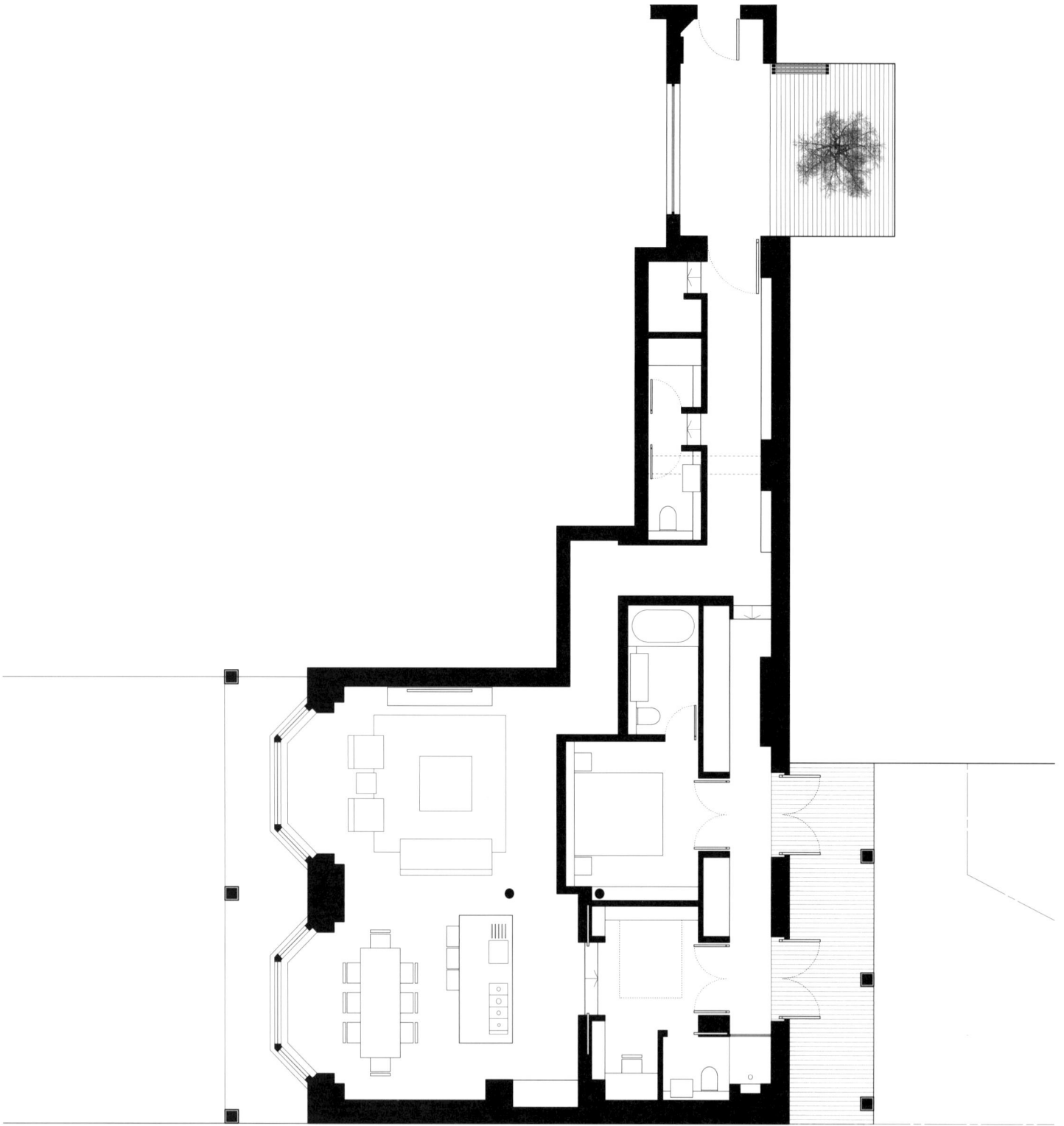

Floor plan of the
remodelled apartment

SALCOTT ROAD

Giles & Pike have added a contemporary wing to the side of this end-of-terrace house in Battersea. This new addition has dramatically increased the space within the house, both at ground and first floor levels, and has created some dynamic new open-plan accommodation. An exposed steel beam and a band of clerestory glazing separate the ground and first floor extensions, providing a strong feature along the new flank wall.

Side elevation to the
Salcott Road house

Salcott Road

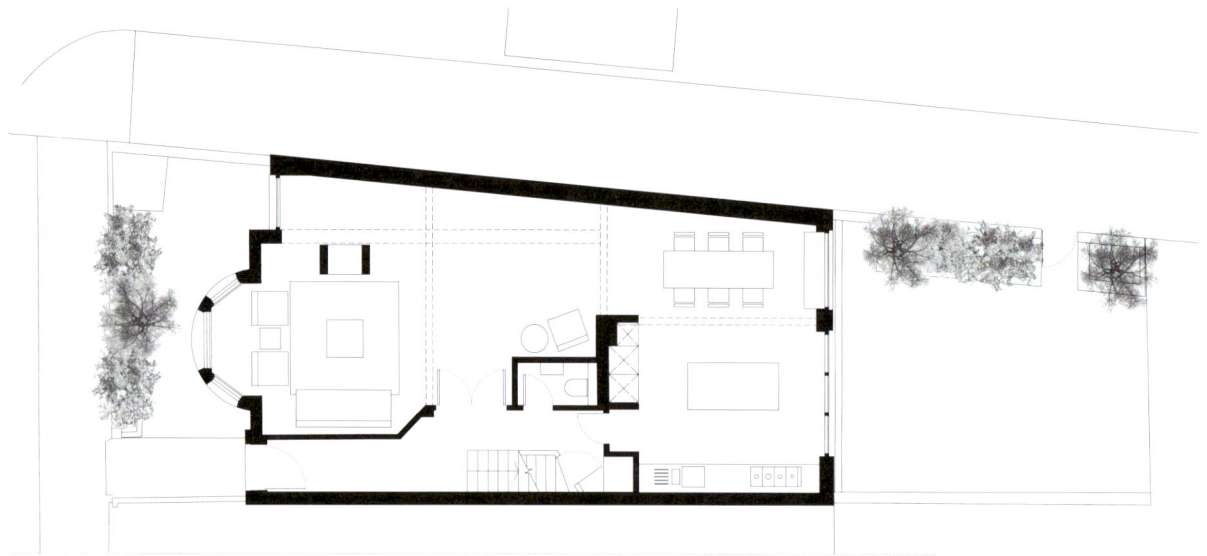

Floor plan of Salcott Road

View across the main living area

Views across the open-plan
side extension areas

Red brickwork pilasters
structuring the new
rear extension

THURLEIGH ROAD (EAST)

In the redesign and remodelling process, the interior spaces at Thurleigh Road have been opened up considerably, creating some dynamic vistas through the house. The rear ground-floor section of the house forms an extremely spacious kitchen, dining area and living room, where family life takes place. The new extension at the rear, which is framed with red brick columns, creates a strong rear facade and acts as a sympathetic foil to the existing fabric of the late-Victorian building.

Rear elevation drawing
with the rear extension

Thurleigh Road (East)

Views of the dining room
and living room in the
new open-plan extension

Thurleigh Road (East)

MELODY ROAD

An inner courtyard has been created for this terraced house just off Wandsworth Common. This has two distinct benefits: it allows natural light to penetrate deep into the property and it also separates the main living area from the kitchen and dining room, affording dynamic vistas across the courtyard from one space to the other. On the top floor, the loft space has been imaginatively reconstructed with an angled, glazed wall of structural glass facing the rear garden. Not only does this create an interesting roofscape, but it allows for spectacular views across this part of London.

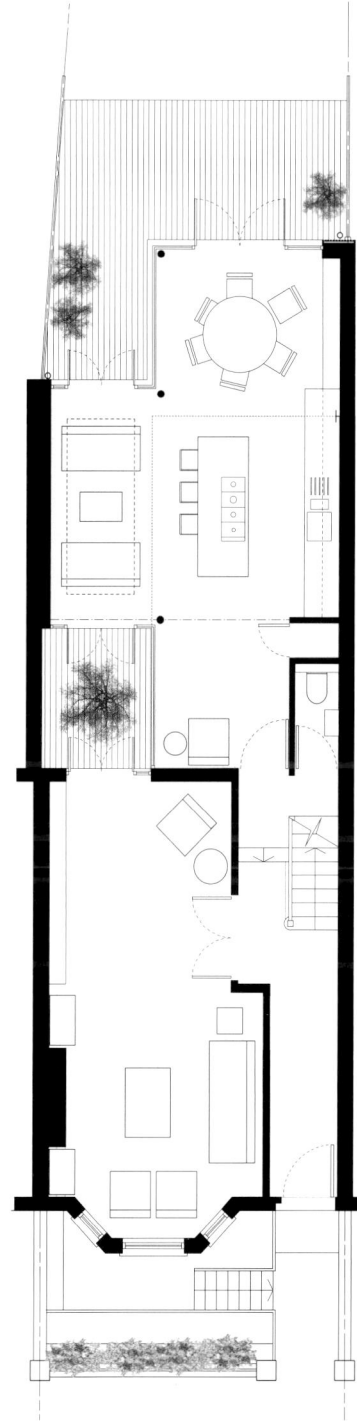

Opposite: A bright blue column
supports the new extension

Floor plan showing the opened-
up kitchen / dining areas

Top: Eaves detail

View into the new
extension at dusk

Melody Road

SPENCER ROAD

Spencer Road is an excellent example of an imposing Victorian villa in south-west London. Giles & Pike had the opportunity to reinvent this property and make many improvements and additions on a bold scale. It is now a decidedly 'Modern Movement' house within the confines of a Victorian-built envelope. A double-height space has been created at the back of the house, connecting the living room, dining room, kitchen and study.

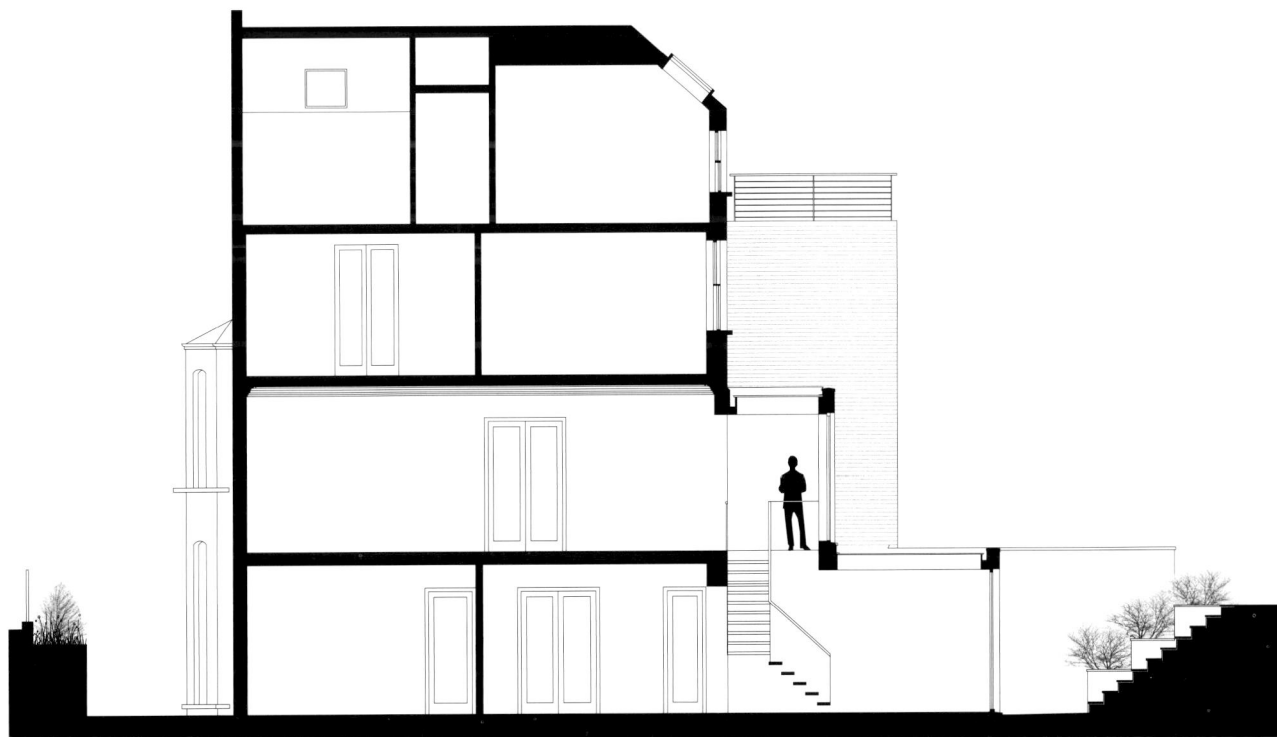

Opposite: The back of
the house at dusk

Cross section through the house

Spencer Road

View to the landscaped garden

Views across the double-height rear extension

Spencer Road

An orange-painted cruciform
column supports the new
roof structure

BRODRICK ROAD

The owners of this house in Wandsworth had previously built
a new extension to the side and rear of their property but they
were never really satisfied with the end result. So, after careful
deliberation they made a bold move to commission Giles &
Pike Architects to start over again from scratch. This involved
demolishing the existing extension and redesigning a new one.
The resulting scheme involved the total remodelling of the back of
the house, and the construction of a sharp new extension, made
almost entirely of glass. The steel structure for the extension has
been carefully designed and exposed, and painted bright orange
so as to create a dynamic structural focus and accent point.

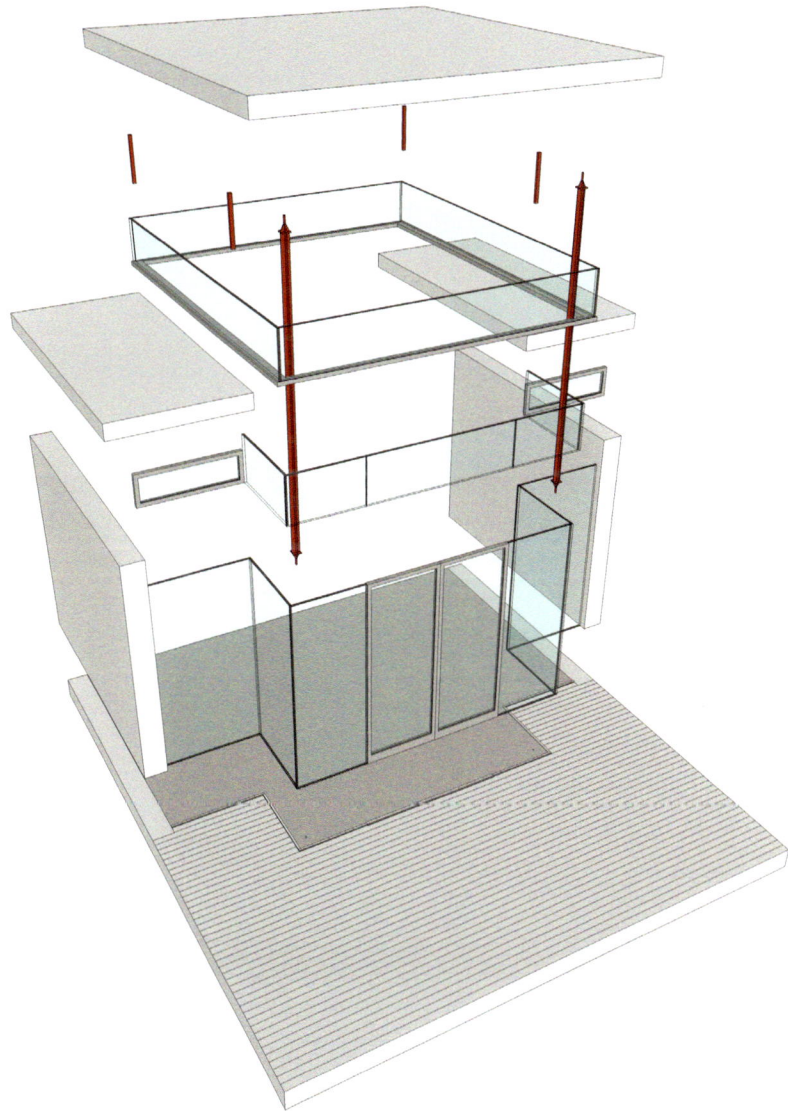

Exploded diagram of
the new structure

Brodrick Road

Detail of the cruciform column

The kitchen area from
the new glazed extension

129   Brodrick Road

Opposite: View of the structurally
glazed exterior from the terrace

Pencil-point detail at base
of the columns

EARLY WORK
1983–1999

Interior view of the Francis
Graham-Dixon Gallery

View of the Ogilvy & Mather video
production studios

OGILVY & MATHER

In the years 1983 to 1990, the practice designed many schemes for the agency Ogilvy & Mather's new offices in Clerkenwell, a video recording studio in Covent Garden, and many office schemes, reception areas, conference rooms and entertaining areas at the head office overlooking the Thames at Waterloo Bridge. The Ogilvy house rules were to achieve clean uncluttered space, being stylish and exciting without resorting to any form of design gimmick or cliché. The work produced for Ogilvy's during this period of the 1980s worked well with the ethos of the company, and the aesthetics were derived from both a functional discipline and an imaginative use of materials.

Reception area in one of Ogilvy's
satellite offices in Clerkenwell

Ogilvy & Mather

Exterior and interior
views of the gallery

FRANCIS GRAHAM-DIXON GALLERY

In 1989 Francis Graham-Dixon, one of London's leading contemporary art dealers at the time, opened a new gallery in Great Sutton Street, Clerkenwell.

The project involved the conversion of a Victorian building that had previously been used as a metal workshop. The rugged industrial nature of the building was stripped back, and then sensitively and inexpensively fitted out as a series of sleek gallery spaces. A new staircase was designed to open up the basement and allow visual access from the pavement into the lower gallery. Minimalist detailing and a clearly defined space help to present the gallery's work in the best possible light.

This project helped spark the regeneration of Clerkenwell at the end of the 1980s.

Lower level gallery, upper gallery
and the new connecting stairs

New glazed entrance area to
Asylum's offices and workshops

ASYLUM

Asylum is a unique company that creates special effects for the television and film industry—the *Star Wars* films and the BBC Two logos are two of their most notable assignments. In 1996 they moved to a new industrial complex in Wandsworth and commissioned Giles & Pike Architects to create a master plan for the site and to build a new workshop to house their fibreglass and moulded plastics processes.

The new building, which has an exposed steel frame and is clad in corrugated steel panels, was cited by CABE (Commission for Architecture and the Built Environment) as one of the most successful industrial buildings of its era.

Interior views of the Asylum
offices and meeting area

The new plastics workshop where
GRP models are fabricated

Overleaf: The new steel-framed
workshops for Asylum, at their
Wandsworth factory site

141   Asylum

SURREY HOUSE

Surrey House is built on a sloping site in a secluded wooded part of Surrey, with views over the rural landscape. This new house was conceived by Giles & Pike to take maximum advantage of its location.

It was designed in the late 1990s and built just before the millennium. The practice has employed large areas of glazed curtain walling to bring light into the house and to afford spectacular views. Curved roof structures ripple over one another to add a lyrical element to the scheme, as well as reflecting the rolling nature of the landscape.

Opposite: Industrial building technology evident in the house in the Surrey hills

Triple-height space in the main living room of this modernist house

Interior view of the main
hall showing the exposed
steel structure

RICHMOND GYM

Richmond Gymnastics Association (RGA) is one of the UK's premier gymnastics clubs, training young gymnasts up to Olympic standards.

When Giles & Pike were introduced to the RGA, they were without a home base and were using school and church halls for their training sessions. They initially assisted them in finding a suitable location for their new gymnasium and then put together a successful lottery funding bid and project-managed the whole scheme through to completion. In this sense it was much more than an architectural project, with the practice developing new expertise in the process.

The finished building has proved to be a highly successful facility. When it was opened in 1999 by the Chair of Sport England, he praised the building and stated that it was the most successful sports venue he had seen since lottery funding had become available.

View of the new gymnasium
from the playing fields

Richmond Gym

THE GLASSHOUSE

The Glasshouse is a sophisticated quality operation owned by restaurateur Nigel Platts-Martin. It is less formal than its sister establishment, The Square, owing to its location in the residential area of Kew. It is a no-frills restaurant of exceptional quality, which is a firm favourite in south-west London.

The interior is a clean, uncluttered dining room, a dynamic space that places emphasis on the presentation and service of the excellent cuisine. The design of the frontage incorporates sliding folding glazed doors, enabling the restaurant to open up in the summer months and customers to spill out on to the pavement. The Glasshouse established itself quickly on the restaurant scene and has won several prestigious restaurant awards, as well as a coveted Michelin star.

Opposite: Interior of the new restaurant, with generous areas of glazing to the facade

Exterior views of the restaurant

Entrance to The Square with
a curvilinear glass canopy

THE SQUARE

Co-owned by Nigel Platts-Martin and Philip Howard, The Square is a destination restaurant with an international reputation. In 1997, Giles & Pike Architects assisted with the relocation of the restaurant to larger, more prestigious Mayfair premises and then managed the redesign of the new restaurant.

The architectural treatment of the building and its presentation to the street are of a sophisticated and timeless quality. The project represents an excellent example of how haute cuisine, superb service and high-quality design can come together to give the customer an all-round experience.

Frontage to the restaurant
with columns and pilasters
clad in black granite

BIOGRAPHIES

Matthew Giles BA, Dip Arch RIBA

Matthew studied architecture at Liverpool Polytechnic, the University of Washington and the University of Liverpool, graduating in 1996. Whilst a student architect Matthew was employed by shedkm in Liverpool, where he worked on a number of urban renewal schemes including the first Urban Splash development Concert Square apartments.

After graduating, Matthew spent three years working in Miami and the Caribbean as a project architect responsible for several hotel developments.

On returning to London at the end of 1999, Matthew worked for United Designers, overseeing and designing high-end residential projects including a house for Bruce Willis. During his time at United, Matthew was also responsible for the winning entry for No. 1 Glasgow, a city-centre hotel in the former Glasgow Post Office building on George Square.

In 2002, Matthew joined The Pike Practice and now designs and manages multiple residential projects, both new build and refurbishments. Matthew became a partner in 2008 and the firm was renamed Giles & Pike Architects in 2010.

Matthew lives with his wife Liza and their two sons in Peckham; he is a keen collector of contemporary art and also enjoys cooking, playing football and making models with his boys.

Tom Pike Dip AD, Dip Arch RIBA

Tom has had a long and fulfilling career in architecture and design, during which he has been involved with a wide variety of disciplines.

Tom studied fine art and 3D design at Farnham School of Art and then went on to study architecture at Kingston University. On graduating in 1978, he co-founded the architectural and interior design practice of Tilney Pike Shane. The firm flourished during the 1980s and soon became one of London's forefront practices involved in commercial interior design.

Tom started up The Pike Practice in 1987 and began to focus more on architectural work. The firm enjoyed a sustained period of growth, both in scale and in the breadth of projects.

In 2008, Tom went into partnership with Matthew Giles and the practice changed its name to Giles & Pike Architects in 2010.

Away from the office, Tom's passions lie in both art and sport. He is a part-time painter, an art collector, a cricketer, tennis player and a keen follower of rugby and football.

Edwina Threipland MA Cantab, Dip Arch RIBA

Edwina studied architecture at Cambridge University, London Metropolitan University and Westminster University.

During her studies Edwina travelled to Malaysia, working on high-end residences and commercial projects in Bangkok, Singapore and Kuala Lumpur.

She became interested in climate change and related issues and worked with Raoul Bunschoten in his urban master-planning studio, specialising in housing that mitigated its environmental impact through floodwater manipulation and renewable energies.

On graduation, Edwina pursued her interests in climate-related design and joined ZEDfactory, where she ran new-build projects that achieved zero carbon ratings and ecological refurbishments of existing housing stock. Edwina moved on to KSR Architects where she became a team leader responsible for matters relating to sustainability and green design. Edwina joined Giles & Pike in 2010.

Away from the office, she has recently completed a house for her family in Spain, using full-height glazing with spectacular views over mountains and sea. She is also interested in theatre and enjoys writing on architectural matters and ecological issues.

Ellen Sacks-Jones BA AA, Dipl RIBA

Whilst studying architecture at Newcastle University, Ellen also worked for the renowned northern firm of FaulknerBrowns on sports-related projects, hotel schemes and in the educational unit. After her time in Newcastle, she moved back to London and continued her education at the Architectural Association where she completed her Part III.

In 2008 she joined the firm BHM Architects, where she qualified. Whilst there she worked largely on educational projects, including an academy school in west London. Ellen joined Giles & Pike in 2010 and soon became an important member of the team.

Ellen has a particular interest in designing educational environments. As a student, she was involved in an architecture programme for schools, which encouraged children to take an interest in the built environment.

Ellen has curated architecture exhibitions and has written various articles for the RIBA Journal. Her interests outside the office lie in travel and the theatre.

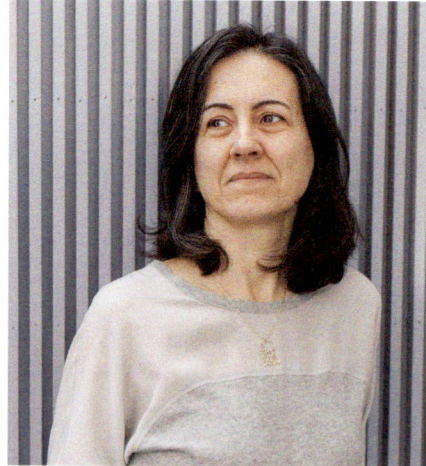

Kate Yaldren

Kate completed a foundation course at Winchester School of Art in 1991. She then went on to do a Higher National Diploma course in shoe design and millinery at Cordwainers College. On graduation she joined Coexistence, where she worked on the sales side of the company. She then moved on to SCP where she managed the Shoreditch showroom and acted as the accessory buyer.

In 2007 she joined Inform Furniture, where she worked on both the selection and the specification of Scandinavian furniture. She also assisted on the project management and installation side of the business.

In 2008, Kate joined Giles & Pike where she is overall practice manager and has helped develop to her project management services.

Paula Bridges BA Arch, MSc RIBA

Paula grew up and was educated in Brazil, graduating in architecture from the Federal University of Minas Gerais. Arriving in Britain in 1993, she settled in Edinburgh, and worked for several practices there, as well as taking an MSc in Computer Aided Building Design at Strathclyde University.

In 1997, Paula came to London and worked for The Halpern Partnership (now Formation Architects). The most significant project she worked on was the refurbishment of the Langham Hotel in Portland Place, including the design of a new leisure complex.

Paula joined The Pike Practice in 2002 and since then has been a key member of the team. She has been responsible for some of Giles & Pike's most significant projects and has recently headed up the project team on the St Mary's Road project—a major new-build house in Wimbledon.

As well as her interests in architecture, Paula is keen to improve her windsurfing skills, take a photography course and to learn more foreign languages.

William Parker BA Arch, MA Arts and Space MSA

William studied for his BA in Architectural Design at the Manchester School of Architecture, obtaining a first class honours degree in 2014. During his final year his design focus was within the atelier "Adaptive Architecture for Climate Change", and through this he developed a keen interest in sustainable and nature-inclusive design.

After his studies in Manchester, William took some time to work within another passion of his: contemporary art. He spent two years operating in production at a project space in Mayfair, as well as opening a small residency programme and construction installation for international galleries at art fairs such as Frieze London.

Alongside this he completed a Masters in Art and Space at Kingston University before joining Giles & Pike in early 2017, on his placement year as a student architect.

William is also a keen traveller. Most recently he redesigned and converted an American school bus into a motorhome, before completing a trip across the United States.

Pamela Wilcox BA Arch (Hons), DipArch ARB

Pamela grew up and was educated in Zimbabwe and after school she studied architecture at The Mackintosh School of Art in Glasgow. She completed her professional qualifications at the Bartlett School of Architecture, UCL.

She worked for many years for Hunt Thompson Associates in Camden, working on social housing programmes, and subsequently at Paul Archer Design in Farringdon.

Pamela has wide-ranging skills and interests in architecture, but one of her main areas of concern is translating our knowledge and expertise in sustainability in the West and using this to solve environmental problems in the developing world.

As well as designing buildings, Pamela has a working knowledge and experience in the building process and has taken courses in various building trades. She has used her craft skills to build her own house.

CREDITS AND ACKNOWLEDGEMENTS

Dominic Bradbury is a freelance writer and journalist specialising in architecture and design. He contributes to many magazines and newspapers in the UK and internationally, including *The Times*, *The Telegraph*, *The Financial Times*, *World of Interiors*, *Wallpaper**, *House & Garden*, *Architectural Digest* and many others. He has written over 20 books on design, interiors and architecture and has collaborated with a number of leading publishers including Thames & Hudson, Conran Octopus and Rizzoli. Bradbury's titles include *Mid-Century Modern Complete*, *The Iconic House: Architectural Masterworks Since 1900* and *The Iconic Interior: 1900 to the Present*. He lives in Norfolk with his wife and three children.

Structural Engineers:
Giles & Pike Architects would like to acknowledge the contribution that the structural engineers have made to the work featured in this book. The structural engineering has played a crucial role in most of the projects. In particular thanks go to the following:

Timothy George
Tom Watson, Tom Steel and Duncan Walters
of Heyne Tillett Steel
Tony Hayes and Jonathan Coleman
of The Michael Barclay Partnership
Sinclair Johnston and Kevin Hallaway
of Sinclair Johnston and Partners

The photographers whose work is featured in this book:
Edmund Sumner
Logan Irvine-MacDougall
John Riddy
Winfried Heinze
Jacob Sacks-Jones
Jasper Fry